10 9 8 7 6 5 4 3 2 1   10 9 8 7 6 5 4 3 2 1 (Pbk)

Library of Congress Cataloging in Publication Data, ISBN: 0-671-64567-6, ISBN; 0-671-66340-2 (Pbk)

Silverman, Maida. Festival of freedom: the story of Passover / retold by Maida Silverman; illustrated by Carolyn S. Ewing. 32 p.
Summary: Retells the story of the Israelites' fight for liberation from slavery in Egypt and presents recipes used in celebrating that
occasion, Passover; a song; and instructions for a traditional seder. ISBN 0-671-64567-6. 1. Passover — Juvenile literature. 2. Seder
— Juvenile literature. [1. Passover. 2. Seder.] I. Ewing, C. S., ill. II. Title. BM695.P3S48 1988   296.4'37 — dc19   87-30388
CIP AC

The author wishes to thank Ms. Judith Muffs of the Anti-Defamation League of B'nai Brith for her assistance, and for providing Dayenu.

FESTIVAL
of FREEDOM

THE STORY OF PASSOVER

RETOLD BY MAIDA SILVERMAN
ILLUSTRATED BY CAROLYN S. EWING

A Little Simon Book
Published by Simon & Schuster, Inc.

Long ago, the Children of Israel came to Egypt because there was famine in their land. They were a small group, only seventy people. They needed food, and pasture for their sheep and goats. Pharoah, the Egyptian king, was kind to them. He gave the Israelites fine land to settle on. They were allowed to pray to their own God and live as they pleased.

Many years passed. A new, cruel Pharoah ruled Egypt. "The Israelites have grown in strength and number," he said. "They might rise against us, or join our enemies and make war. I must find a way to control them."

Pharoah took away the Israelites' possessions. He forced them to make bricks and mortar to build his cities, and filled their days with hard labor. Their lives as Pharoah's slaves were bitter, and they cried out to God for help.

One day, the royal fortunetellers came to Pharoah. "A great Israelite leader will soon be born," they told him. "He will lead his people to freedom in a new land."

Pharoah was furious. He wanted to keep his slaves. He ordered all male Israelite babies to be drowned as soon as they were born.

Not long after Pharoah's cruel decree, an Israelite woman named Yocheved gave birth to a son. She hid her baby at home as long as she could. Then she laid him in a little basket and hid him among the reeds that grew along the Nile river.

Pharoah's daughter came to bathe in the river. She found the infant and took pity on him. She named him Moses and raised him in the palace as if he were her child, but he knew he was a child of Israel. His people's sufferings filled him with grief.

One day, while tending sheep near Mt. Horeb, Moses saw a wondrous sight. A bush burned on the mountainside, but was not destroyed. God's voice spoke to Moses from the midst of the flames.

"Go to Pharoah," He said. "Tell him to let my people go!"

Moses did as the Lord asked. But Pharoah liked having slaves to command. He refused.

"God will punish you and the Egyptians," Moses warned.

"I do not know your God," Pharoah answered. "I am not afraid of Him!"

And so God sent ten plagues into Egypt. First He turned all the waters into blood. Fish died, and there was no water to drink. Then God sent a plague of frogs. They climbed out of the rivers and swarmed everywhere. God turned the dust of earth into millions of gnats that bit the Egyptians. But Pharoah would not free the Israelites.

God sent clouds of flies into Egypt and ruined the land. He sent sickness to the cattle, and inflicted sores on the bodies of the Egyptians. But Pharoah still would not let the Israelites go.

God sent fiery hail that crushed the barley and flax. He sent swarms of locusts that devoured whatever the hail had spared. Then God sent a great darkness. It covered all of Egypt, and the Egyptians could not leave their houses. But Pharoah was stubborn. He said, "I will not free the Israelites!"

God spoke again to Moses. "I will send the most terrible plague of all to Egypt. Only then will Pharaoh let my people go."

Moses went to the elders of Israel and told them what to do. "This night, the Angel of Death will pass over the land. You shall sacrifice a lamb, and sprinkle its blood on the doorposts of your house. The Angel of Death will see the blood, and spare your family. But he will strike down the eldest sons of the Egyptians. Even Pharoah's son shall die."

All happened as Moses foretold. Pharoah was terrified. He ordered the Israelites to leave Egypt at once. They even had to take the bread dough, for there was no time to let it rise or bake. Moses led his people out of Egypt, and God went before them in a pillar of smoke by day and a pillar of fire at night.

Before very long Pharoah was sorry he had freed the Israelites. "Why should I lose so many slaves?" he said. Pharoah ordered his army to find the Israelites and bring them back to Egypt.

Moses and his people had come to the shore of the Red Sea. When they saw Pharoah's chariots and soldiers, they cried out in terror. The Israelites were trapped between the Egyptian army and the sea.

God told Moses, "Stretch your hand over the sea. The waters will divide, and my people shall walk on dry ground."

Moses did as God commanded. The Israelites crossed safely to the other side. Pharoah's soldiers pursued them. When they were halfway across, God told Moses to stretch forth his hand once more. The sea closed up, drowning the armies of Pharaoh. The Israelites joyfully praised the Lord.

Moses said, "Never forget that once you were slaves in Egypt, set free by God. For seven days, you shall eat unleavened bread, because we took unleavened bread with us in our haste, and

baked it in the desert. Remember how the Angel of Death passed over us and struck down the first-born sons of the Egyptians. Keep the Passover in its season, from this day forward."

Passover has been celebrated for more than 3,000 years. The holiday begins on the 15th of the Hebrew month of *Nisan* (usually in April). It is called *Pesach* or Passover because the Angel of Death "passed over" the Israelites' houses when he smote the first-born sons of the Egyptians. Passover is a holiday especially for children, for it is said in the Holy Books: "You shall tell your children the story of Passover."

The Seder is a traditional meal eaten on the first and second nights of Passover. Friends, family and even the littlest children gather together to tell and remember the miracles God performed for his people.

The Seder Plate is put on the table. On the plate are six special foods that will be explained during the Seder.

A platter holding three matzot (unleavened bread) is placed on the table also. Matza, a flat, cracker-like bread made only with flour and water, symbolizes the unleavened bread eaten by the Israelites. In their haste to leave Egypt, there was no time for the bread to rise.

The *Haggadah* is a book that tells the story of Passover. It also tells what to do during the Seder. Everyone reads from it during the Seder service.

THE SEDER PLATE

The Seder plate is a large platter. On it are placed:

A ROASTED BONE: This stands for the sacrificial lamb, offered by the Israelites on the evening of the departure from Egypt.

A ROASTED EGG: Symbolizes a Festival Offering brought to the Holy Temple in ancient times.

MAROR: Bitter herbs, usually horseradish root and romaine or endive lettuce. They symbolize the bitterness of slavery.

HAROSET: A mixture of fruit, cinnamon, nuts and wine, haroset symbolizes the bricks and mortar the Israelites were forced to make for Pharoah.

KARPAS: Parsley or watercress, suggesting the first greens of spring.

SALT WATER: A reminder of the tears of sorrow shed by the Israelites when they were slaves.

THE SEDER

The Seder begins with a blessing, *Kiddush*, said by the Seder leader.

Sprigs of parsley or watercress are dipped into salt water, blessed and eaten by all. Then the Seder leader breaks one matza into two pieces. The larger piece, called the Afikomen, or "dessert," is wrapped in a napkin and hidden.

The leader holds up the plate of matzot and says: "This is the bread of affliction, which our ancestors ate in the land of Egypt. Let all who are hungry come and eat. Let all who wish to come and celebrate the Passover."

The youngest child now asks the Four Questions:

Why is this night different from all other nights? Why on this night do we eat only matza?

Why on this night do we eat only bitter herbs?

On all other nights we do not even dip once. Why on this night do we dip twice?

Why on this night do we eat reclining?

The Questions are answered:

We eat matza to remember that our ancestors, in their haste to leave Egypt, could not wait for the bread to rise.

We eat bitter herbs to remember the bitterness of slavery.

We dip greens in salt water to replace tears with thankfulness and we dip bitter herbs in haroset (a fruit mixture) because the bitterness of slavery was sweetened by God's rescue.

On this night we show our freedom by reclining. In ancient Egypt, only free men could do this.

The leader blesses the matza and all are given a piece to eat. A prayer is said and everyone eats bitter herbs with haroset. Then everyone makes a sandwich of bitter herbs, haroset, and matza.

After a holiday dinner is served, the children are sent to look for the Afikomen. When the Afikomen is found, the leader gives everyone a piece to eat as dessert.

A cup of wine is filled for the prophet Elijah, God's messenger of hope and peace. The door is opened for him, and he is invited to join the feast with a prayer of welcome. The children watch Elijah's cup, sure the prophet has visited them and sipped from his cup. Songs are sung and stories told, and so the Seder is

HAROSET, EASTERN EUROPEAN STYLE

3 apples, peeled, cored
   and chopped

$\frac{1}{2}$ cup sweet red wine or grape juice

$\frac{1}{2}$ teaspoon powdered
   cinnamon

$\frac{3}{4}$ cup chopped almonds

Mix apples with wine or grape juice and cinnamon, mashing slightly with a fork. Add almonds and blend well. Add a few spoonfuls of liquid, if needed. Store in refrigerator.

HAROSET, ISRAELI STYLE

1 ripe banana, peeled

10 soft pitted dates, chopped

$\frac{1}{2}$ cup golden raisins, chopped

1 apple, peeled, cored and chopped

$\frac{1}{2}$ teaspoon powdered
   cinnamon

$\frac{1}{2}$ cup sweet red wine or
   grape juice

$\frac{1}{2}$ cup chopped walnuts

Mix fruit, cinnamon and wine or grape juice. Stir in walnuts. Add a few spoonfuls of wine or grape juice if mixture seems too stiff. Store in refrigerator.

DAYENU

Dayenu (da-yay-noo) is a song of thanksgiving, almost 1,500 years old. Dayenu means "it would have been enough." Any one of the miracles God performed for His people would have been enough, but for each one, His people are grateful. Dayenu is sung during the Seder.

FOLK SONG